Reptiles

Catriona Clarke

Designed by Will Dawes

Illustrated by Connie McLennan

Additional illustrations by Tim Haggerty
Additional design by Helen Edmonds and John Russell
Reptile consultant: Dr. Tobias Uller, University of Oxford
Reading consultant: Alison Kelly, Roehampton University

Contents

Reptiles

Reptiles have lived on Earth for millions and millions of years. Now, there are over 8,000 different types.

This is an Eastern collared lizard. These reptiles are found in North America.

What is a reptile?

There are four main kinds of reptiles.

Crocodiles and alligators are fierce hunters with very powerful tails.

Snakes have slim, bendy bodies and no legs. Most snakes eat bigger animals.

Lizards are usually small, with long tails. They can run very quickly.

Turtles and tortoises have domed shells made up of hard, bony scales.

However different they look, nearly all reptiles...

...have scaly, waterproof skin...

...lay eggs...

...and are cold-blooded. This means that they need the sun's heat to keep their bodies warm.

5

Little and large

Some reptiles are tiny, and some are huge.

A pygmy chameleon can fit on a person's finger.

It eats flies that are almost too small for people to see.

Saltwater crocodiles are big enough to attack sharks!

The Galapagos giant tortoise
is the biggest tortoise
in the world.

It is as big as the wheel of a truck,
and can live for over 100 years.

Reptile homes

Reptiles are able to live in all kinds of different places.

Boomslang snakes live in trees, where they feed on small reptiles and sometimes birds.

Fringe-toed lizards live in sandy deserts where it is very hot during the day.

Gopher tortoises dig burrows in the ground. They stay there most of the time.

Reptiles live everywhere in the world – except for Antarctica where it is too cold for them.

Sea-snakes like this one live around coral reefs in warm oceans.

Hot and cold

A reptile's body doesn't work well when it's too hot or cold. Reptiles spend a lot of time trying to stay at the right temperature.

This marine iguana is basking in the sun after swimming in the cold sea.

1. At dawn, a lizard sits on a sunny rock to warm up after the cold night.

2. It gets very hot in the middle of the day, so the lizard lies under a rock.

3. The lizard hunts for food in the afternoon when its body is working better.

4. The air and rocks get cool at night, so the lizard goes back to its burrow.

When crocodiles get too hot, they open their mouths to cool off.

Scaly skin

Reptiles shed their skin as they grow bigger.

1. A snake's body and eyes start to look dull when it's ready to lose its skin.

2. The snake rubs its head against a rock. The skin splits and starts to come off.

3. Over a few days, the snake's skin peels off slowly in one whole piece.

4. The skin underneath is bright and glossy. The snake will shed again in a few weeks.

Most lizards shed their skin in patches, but this forest gecko is shedding its skin in one piece.

Lots of geckos rip off the outer layer of their skin and then eat it!

Getting around

Lots of reptiles have very unusual ways of moving around.

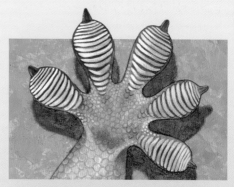

Some geckos climb walls and ceilings in people's houses.

They climb so well because of sticky ridges on their toes.

This lizard is a green basilisk. It can run across water for short distances to escape when it is scared.

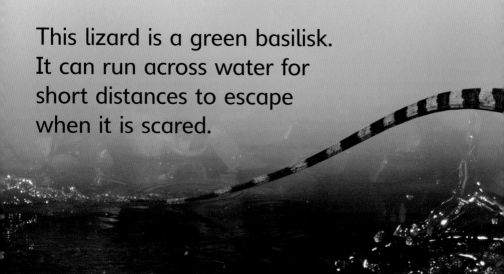

A flying dragon has flaps of skin attached to its tummy.

It can open up the flaps to help it glide from tree to tree.

Special skills

Some reptiles have special skills that help them find things to eat.

A snake can 'taste' the air with its forked tongue.

This tells the snake if there is any prey nearby.

A chameleon can swivel its eyes in different directions at the same time, so it can see all around.

Tokay geckos are nocturnal. This means they are awake at night.

They have very big eyes that help them to find insects in the dark.

The geckos don't have eyelids, so they lick their eyes to clean them.

Hunting for food

Most reptiles hunt other creatures for food.

Chameleons use their long sticky tongues to catch insects.

A crocodile lurks in a river with only its eyes above water.

It suddenly lunges out of the water and grabs a zebra.

An alligator snapping turtle sits on a muddy riverbed with its mouth open.

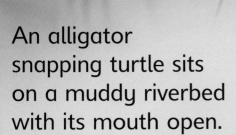

The turtle has a red lump on its tongue that looks like a worm.

A fish tries to eat the 'worm', but the turtle snaps its jaws shut and eats the fish.

A killer bite

Some snakes kill their prey by injecting them with deadly venom.

This is a diamondback rattlesnake.

The snake bites prey with its fangs to inject venom.

Snakes can stretch their mouths to eat
very big prey – including other snakes!

A gaboon viper lies in
wait next to a rabbit
trail until a rabbit
hops past.

The snake attacks.
It bites the rabbit
with its razor-
sharp fangs.

The rabbit hops away, but dies
from the snake's venom.
The snake eats it later.

Blending in

Some reptiles can change the way they look, and some can blend in with their surroundings.

Chameleons can change how their skin looks to show their mood.

This chameleon's bright skin shows that it's angry.

A vine snake's thin green body looks like a vine on a tree.

A sahara sand viper is well camouflaged in the sand.

This frilled gecko looks like a dead leaf.

It is very hard to spot unless it moves.

Under attack

Reptiles often have to protect themselves against bigger animals.

A short-toed eagle swoops down to attack a wall lizard.

The lizard's tail drops off and starts to wriggle. This gives the lizard time to escape.

The lizard's tail grows back later, but the new tail is short and stumpy.

Grass snakes pretend to be dead to make an attacker go away.

A frilled lizard opens up a huge frill around its neck when it is scared. This makes it look bigger, so other animals will leave it alone.

Eggs and babies

Some reptiles look after their babies, but most of them lay eggs and then leave their babies to look after themselves.

A mother alligator looks after her babies for two years.

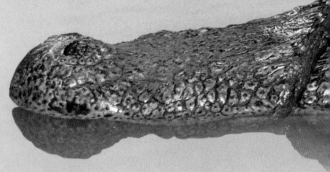

1. A leatherback turtle swims back to the beach where she was born.

2. She digs a hole in the sand with her flippers, then lays her eggs in the hole.

This baby alligator is basking in the sun on its mother's head.

3. The turtle lays about 100 eggs, then she flicks sand over them until they are buried.

4. Two months later, baby turtles hatch from the eggs and scurry to the sea.

Weird reptiles

Some reptiles look strange, or do very strange things.

A gharial is a type of crocodile. It has a very thin snout, and pointy teeth that make it easy to catch small fish.

Horned lizards squirt blood from their eyes to scare away other animals.

Thorny devils are the strangest looking lizards.

They look fierce, but they only eat ants. The spikes on the lizard's body stop other animals from attacking it.

Glossary of reptile words

Here are some of the words in this book you might not know. This page tells you what they mean.

 cold-blooded – an animal that can't produce its own body heat.

 basking – lying in the sun to get warm. Most reptiles do this every day.

 shedding – losing a layer of skin. Most reptiles shed every few months.

 prey – animals that are hunted and eaten by other animals.

 venom – a poisonous liquid that some snakes use to kill their prey.

 fangs – long, sharp teeth. Some snakes inject venom with their fangs.

 camouflage – markings that make a reptile difficult to spot.

Websites to visit

You can visit exciting websites to find out more about reptiles.

To visit these websites, go to the Usborne Quicklinks Website at **www.usborne-quicklinks.com** Read the internet safety guidelines, and then type the keywords "**beginners reptiles**".

The websites are regularly reviewed and the links in Usborne Quicklinks are updated. However, Usborne Publishing is not responsible, and does not accept liability, for the content or availability of any website other than its own. We recommend that children are supervised while on the internet.

This leaf-tailed gecko lives on rainforest trees.

Index

Acknowledgements

Photo credits

The publishers are grateful to the following for permission to reproduce material:
© **Alamy** 20 (Steve Hamblin); © **Ardea** 2-3 (Francois Gohier), 5 (M. Watson), 10 (D. Parier & E. Parier-Cook);
© **CG Textures**, cover; © **CORBIS** cover (Frans Lanting); © **Getty Images** 22 (Kevin Schafer), 29 (Cyril Ruoso/
JH Editorial); © **Minden Pictures** 9 (Fred Bavendam), 18 (Stephen Dalton), 28 (Michael & Patricia Fogden);
© **Nature Picture Library** 13 (Steimer/ARCO), 23 (Nick Garbutt), 26-27 (David Kjaer), 31 (Pete Oxford);
© **Oxford Scientific** 1 (David B. Fleetham), 6 (Mike Powles); © **Photolibrary** 6-7 (Tui de Roy),
14-15 (Joe McDonald), 16 (Joel Sartore), 25 (Belinda Wright).

Every effort has been made to trace and acknowledge ownership of copyright. If any rights have
been omitted, the publishers offer to rectify this in any subsequent editions following notification.